Puggles

by Ruth Owen

PowerKiDS press.

New York

Published in 2013 by The Rosen Publishing Group, Inc.
29 East 21st Street, New York, NY 10010

First Edition

Produced for Rosen by Ruby Tuesday Books Ltd
Editor for Ruby Tuesday Books Ltd: Mark J. Sachner
US Editor: Sara Antill
Designer: Emma Randall

Photo Credits:
Cover, 1, 3, 4–5, 6, 8, 10–11, 12, 14–15, 16, 18–19, 21, 26–27, 29, 30 ©
Shutterstock; 7 © Wikipedia Creative Commons; 9, 20, 22–23 © Istock; 13
© James Tourtellotte, U.S. Customs and Border Protection; 17 © Superstock;
24–25 © FLPA; 28 © Brian Bould Daily Mail.

Library of Congress Cataloging-in-Publication Data

Owen, Ruth, 1967–
 Puggles / by Ruth Owen. — 1st ed.
     p. cm. — (Designer dogs)
 Includes index.
 ISBN 978-1-4488-7858-1 (library binding) — ISBN 978-1-4488-7911-3 (pbk.)
 — ISBN 978-1-4488-7917-5 (6-pack)
 1. Puggle—Juvenile literature. I. Title.
 SF429.P92O94 2013
 636.76—dc23

                                                                        2011052942

Manufactured in the United States of America

CPSIA Compliance Information: Batch #B1S12PK: For Further Information contact Rosen Publishing, New York, New York at 1-800-237-9932

Contents

woof

Meet a Puggle

What is smart, loves people, and has lots of energy? The answer is a puggle.

Puggles are a **crossbreed** dog. This means they are a mixture of two different dog **breeds**, or types. When a pug and a beagle have puppies together, they make puggles!

Puggles love to be outside playing, but they also love to snuggle up on the couch with their owner to watch TV.

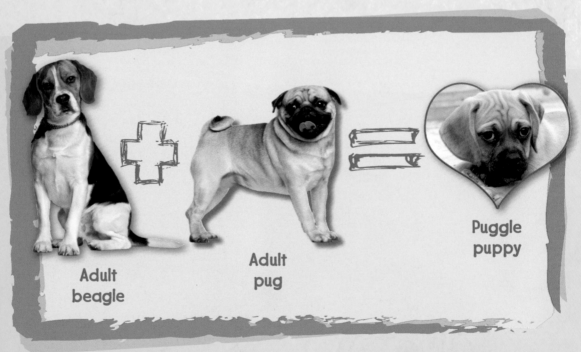

Adult beagle

Adult pug

Puggle puppy

Puggles like to sleep burrowed under blankets or cushions. If their owners want to find them, however, they can listen for some puggle snoring!

A sleeping puggle

5

People, Their Pups, and Puggles

People first began to train wolves and other wild dogs to be pets and working animals over 14,000 years ago. People wanted dogs to do different jobs. So, over many years they mated different types of dogs together to create hundreds of different breeds.

Some dogs were bred to herd sheep and cattle. Many small breeds were created to be pet and **lap dogs** for people. Puggles were created to be pet dogs. The first puggles were bred in the United States, in the 1980s.

Wolf

Great Dane

Chihuahua

A puggle puppy

All dogs, from giant Great Danes to tiny chihuahuas and little puggles, have wild wolves as their **ancestors.**

What Are Designer Dogs?

Some new breeds of dogs that have been created in the past 20 to 30 years have been nicknamed "designer dogs." They get this name because dog breeders designed, or created, them.

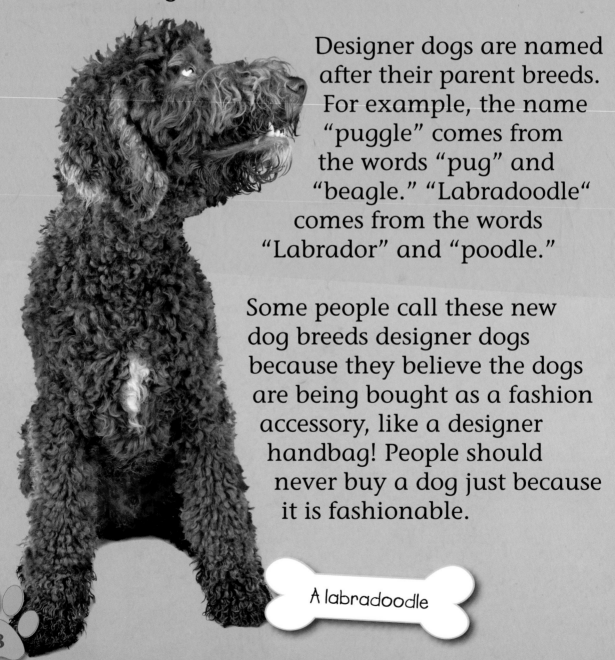

Designer dogs are named after their parent breeds. For example, the name "puggle" comes from the words "pug" and "beagle." "Labradoodle" comes from the words "Labrador" and "poodle."

Some people call these new dog breeds designer dogs because they believe the dogs are being bought as a fashion accessory, like a designer handbag! People should never buy a dog just because it is fashionable.

A labradoodle

Sadly, many puggles and other designer dogs end up in **rescue shelters** needing a home. When owners become bored with their fashionable pet or cannot take care of it properly, the dog is given to a rescue shelter.

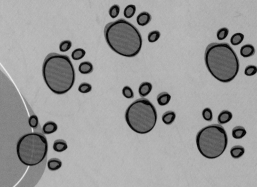

A puggle puppy in a rescue shelter

Meet the Parents: Beagles

Beagles are very active dogs. They need more than two hours of exercise each day!

Beagles have an excellent sense of smell. They were originally bred to work in **packs**, or groups, helping their owners hunt rabbits and hares.

A beagle sniffs the ground to pick up the **scent** of a rabbit. Then the beagle follows the scent trail and leads the human hunter to the **prey**.

Adult beagle size

Weight = approximately 22 pounds (10 kg)

Height = up to 15 inches (38 cm) to the shoulder

When a beagle finds an animal's scent, it barks to tell the other pack members. Then the whole pack follows the trail!

A young beagle follows a scent trail

Meet the Parents: Beagle Brigade

Today, some beagles use their sense of smell to help the US government!

It is against the law to bring meat, fruit, or vegetables into the United States from other countries. This is because these products may carry diseases or insects that could harm farm animals and crops in the United States.

The Beagle Brigade of sniffer beagles works at airports sniffing passengers' luggage. If a beagle smells something suspicious in a suitcase, it shows its human handler by sitting next to the luggage. Then the handler can search the suitcase.

Beagle puppies

The Beagle Brigade dogs are trained to recognize about 50 different smells.

A Beagle Brigade dog sniffs luggage at an airport.

13

Meet the Parents: Pugs

Pugs are often called "toy" dogs. This means they are a small dog breed.

Pugs have a solid, almost rectangular body. Their short, glossy hair can be fawn, black, silver, or an apricot color.

The thing that makes a pug stand out from the crowd is its face. Pugs have very short, flat-looking muzzles. They have large nostrils, a wrinkled forehead, and big, dark eyes.

Adult pug size

Weight = approximately 16 pounds (7 kg)

Black pug

Height = around 12 inches (30 cm) to the shoulder

Fawn pug

Wrinkles

Muzzle

Cheerful, smart pugs love to be around people and want nothing more than to please their humans!

15

Meet the Parents: Pug Royalty

Throughout their history, pugs have been a favorite dog of emperors, kings, and queens! In China, over 2,400 years ago, pugs were the lap dogs of Chinese emperors. Then traders took pugs to Europe.

In 1572, the Dutch prince, William of Orange, was saved by his pug, Pompey. During a war with Spain, Spanish assassins were sent to murder the prince in his tent near the battlefield. Legend says that when the murderers got close to the prince's tent, Pompey jumped on his sleeping master to wake him and warn him of the danger!

A pug puppy

Britain's Queen Victoria bred pugs. She had pet pugs named Basco, Venus, Fatima, Minka, Pedro, and Olga.

Puggle Looks

When you look at a puggle, you can see clues that its parents were a beagle and a pug!

A puggle has a wrinkled forehead like a pug. It has a long muzzle and floppy ears, however, like a beagle.

Puggles have a beagle-shaped body, but short legs, like a pug. Their tails are long like a beagle's, but with a cute, pug-like curl!

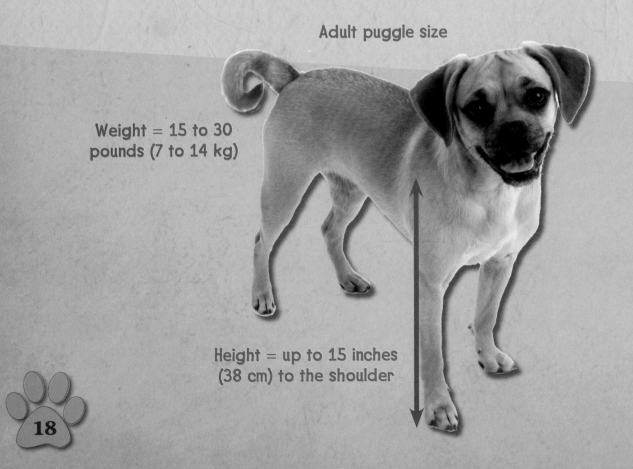

Adult puggle size

Weight = 15 to 30 pounds (7 to 14 kg)

Height = up to 15 inches (38 cm) to the shoulder

Puggles have short hair that can be fawn, brown, black, white, or a mix of these colors. Their faces can be completely black, or have black patches.

19

Friendly, Busy Puggles

Puggles are very affectionate dogs. They **bond** with their human families and want to be near them at all times. Puggles get along well with other dogs and pets, too. They especially like to make new doggie friends at the park.

Puggles enjoy investigating new smells. Like their beagle parents, they have a very good sense of smell and will follow scents along the ground.

A puggle with its best pug friend

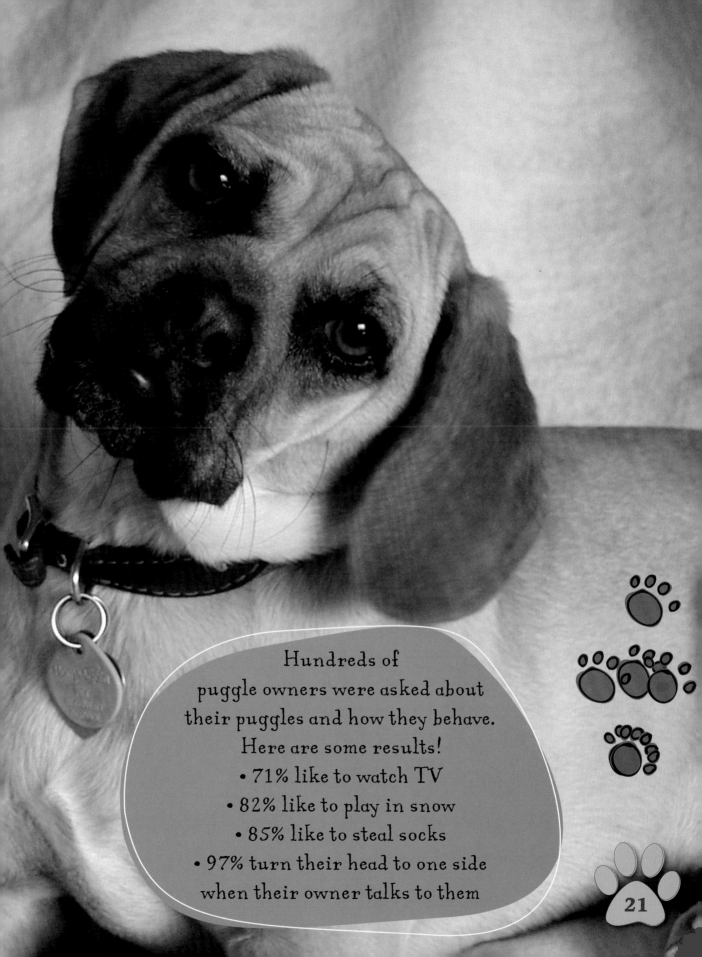

Hundreds of
puggle owners were asked about
their puggles and how they behave.
Here are some results!
- 71% like to watch TV
- 82% like to play in snow
- 85% like to steal socks
- 97% turn their head to one side
when their owner talks to them

21

Moms and Babies

Puggle puppies usually have a beagle mom and a pug dad. The beagle mom gives birth to a **litter** of around four puppies.

When the puppies are born, their eyes are closed. They don't open their eyes until they are about 12 days old. The newborn puggles sleep and drink milk from their mom.

At four weeks old, the puppies begin to play and scamper around!

A beagle mom play-fights with her puggle puppy.

The puppies in a litter can be a mixture of different puggle colors.

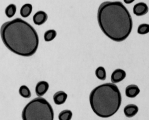

Puggles Growing Up

When a puppy is about four to five weeks old, it can begin to eat solid food. This is called weaning. Dog breeders give their puppies milk and cereal and special canned puppy food.

People who want to own a puggle puppy will visit the breeder to choose a puppy from the litter. When the puggle puppies are eight to ten weeks old, they can go to live with their new human family.

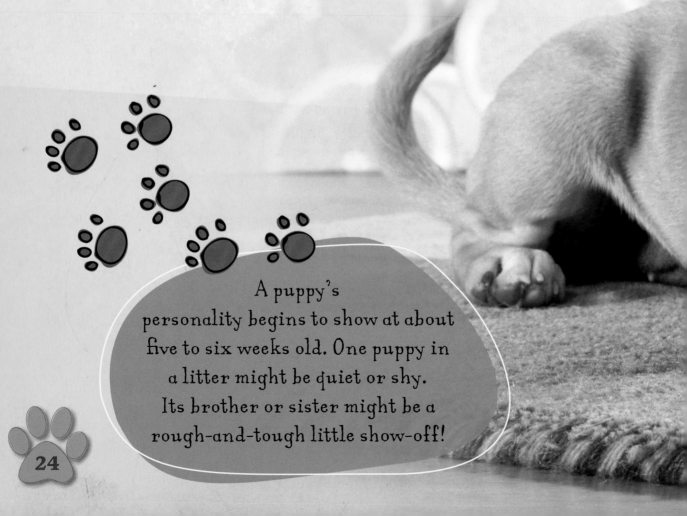

A puppy's personality begins to show at about five to six weeks old. One puppy in a litter might be quiet or shy. Its brother or sister might be a rough-and-tough little show-off!

A puggle puppy

Pet Puggles

A puggle's beauty routine should include having its hair brushed once a week. Its face wrinkles should also be cleaned with a damp cloth. Every few days, a puggle will need to have its teeth brushed.

A puggle should have a 30-minute walk every day. Visiting a dog park to meet and play with other dogs will also keep a puggle fit and happy.

Puggles can eat a lot. If food is left lying around the house, a puggle will soon sniff out a sneaky, extra meal!

A puggle puppy with a bone

Operation Rescue Puggle

In August 2010, three-month-old puggle pup Louis was kidnapped from his garden. After several days, the kidnapper called Louis' owner, Ben. The kidnapper said that if Ben wanted to see Louis again he would have to pay an expensive ransom!

Ben and Louis the puggle

Ben arranged to meet the kidnapper, but he called the police, too. When the kidnapper showed up, a detective pretended to be Ben. As the kidnapper got out of his van, the detective grabbed little Louis. Then police cars surrounded the kidnapper's van so he couldn't escape!

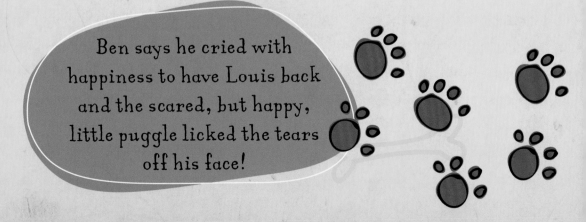

Ben says he cried with happiness to have Louis back and the scared, but happy, little puggle licked the tears off his face!

woof

29

Glossary

ancestor (AN-ses-ter)
A relative who lived long ago.

bond (BOND)
To form a close connection based on love and trust.

breed (BREED)
A type of dog. Also the word used to describe the act of mating two animals in order for them to have young.

crossbreed (KROS-breed)
A type of dog created from two different breeds.

lap dog (LAP DAWG)
A dog that has been bred to be small enough to be carried or to sit on a person's lap.

litter (LIH-ter)
A group of baby animals all born to the same mother at the same time.

pack (PAK)
A group of animals that hunt together.

prey (PRAY)
An animal that is hunted by another animal as food.

rescue shelter (RES-kyoo SHEL-ter)
A place where people take unwanted pets. Workers at a shelter care for the animals and try to find them a new home.

scent (SENT)
A smell left by an animal on the ground or other surface.

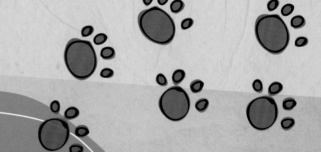

Websites

Due to the changing nature of Internet links, PowerKids Press has developed an online list of websites related to the subject of this book. This site is updated regularly. Please use this link to access the list:

www.powerkidslinks.com/ddog/puggle/

31

Read More

Beal, Abigail. *I Love My Beagle.* Top Dogs. New York: PowerKids Press, 2011.

Landau, Elaine. *Pugs Are the Best!* Best Dogs Ever. Minneapolis, MN: Lerner Publications, 2010.

Wheeler, Jill C. *Puggles.* Minneapolis, MN: Checkerboard Books, 2008.

Index